Marriage and Faith: Finding Spiritual Connection in Your Relationship

There's no denying it: making and keeping happy and healthy relationships is hard.

Table Of Contents

Chapter 1: Understanding the Role of Faith in Marriage

The Importance of Spiritual Connection in a Relationship

In any relationship, whether it be a marriage, a partnership, or a friendship, having a strong spiritual connection can be incredibly important. This connection goes beyond simply sharing the same religious beliefs or attending the same worship services. It involves connecting on a deeper level, spiritually and emotionally, that transcends the physical and material aspects of the relationship.

One of the key reasons why spiritual connection is so important in a relationship is that it provides a sense of shared purpose and meaning. When two people are able to connect on a spiritual level, they are able to support each other in their spiritual journey and growth. This shared sense of purpose can help to strengthen the relationship and provide a solid foundation for facing life's challenges together.

Additionally, spiritual connection can help to foster a sense of trust, intimacy, and emotional connection in a relationship. When two people are able to connect on a spiritual level, they are more likely to be open and vulnerable with each other, sharing their deepest thoughts, fears, and desires. This level of emotional intimacy can help to strengthen the bond between partners and create a deeper sense of connection.

Furthermore, spiritual connection can also provide a source of comfort and support during difficult times. When facing challenges such as financial struggles, mental health issues, infidelity, or communication problems, having a strong spiritual connection can provide a sense of hope and guidance. Partners who are able to draw on their spiritual beliefs and practices in times of need are often better equipped to navigate these challenges together.

Overall, the importance of spiritual connection in a relationship cannot be overstated. Whether you are in a marriage, a partnership, or a friendship, cultivating a strong spiritual connection with your loved one can help to deepen your bond, provide a sense of purpose and meaning, and support you through life's ups and downs.

How Faith Can Strengthen a Marriage

In the subchapter "How Faith Can Strengthen a Marriage," we explore the powerful role that spirituality can play in nurturing and enhancing the bond between partners. For many couples, faith serves as a cornerstone of their relationship, providing a shared set of beliefs and values that guide their interactions and decision-making.

One of the key ways in which faith can strengthen a marriage is by providing a sense of purpose and meaning to the relationship. When couples share a spiritual connection, they are able to draw upon their beliefs to navigate challenges and find deeper fulfillment in their union. This shared sense of purpose can help couples weather the storms of life and grow closer together in the process.

Faith can also provide couples with a sense of hope and resilience in the face of adversity. By turning to their spiritual beliefs during difficult times, couples can find comfort, strength, and guidance to overcome obstacles and emerge stronger on the other side. This sense of faith can help couples maintain a positive outlook on their relationship and work through conflicts with love and understanding.

Furthermore, faith can serve as a source of inspiration for couples to cultivate qualities such as compassion, forgiveness, and gratitude in their marriage. By embodying these values in their relationship, couples can deepen their connection, foster greater intimacy, and build a strong foundation for a lasting partnership.

Ultimately, the role of faith in a marriage is a deeply personal and individual choice. However, for many couples, incorporating spirituality into their relationship can be a powerful tool for deepening their bond, finding meaning and purpose, and navigating the ups and downs of married life with grace and love.

Common Challenges in Maintaining Spiritual Connection

Marriage and Faith: Finding Spiritual Connection in Your Relationship

Maintaining a spiritual connection in a marriage can be challenging due to a variety of factors. One common challenge is the busy and hectic nature of modern life. With work, children, and other responsibilities taking up so much time and energy, finding the time to nurture your spiritual connection can be difficult. It's important to make a conscious effort to prioritize your relationship and set aside time for spiritual practices.

Another challenge is differing beliefs or levels of spiritual commitment between partners. This can lead to conflicts and misunderstandings, especially if one partner feels like their spiritual needs are not being met. It's important to have open and honest communication about your beliefs and values, and to find ways to compromise and support each other's spiritual journeys.

External influences can also pose challenges to maintaining a spiritual connection in a marriage. Family members, friends, and societal pressures can all impact your relationship and spiritual practices. It's important to set boundaries and prioritize your relationship above outside influences.

Financial stress, mental health issues, infidelity, and communication breakdowns can also strain a couple's spiritual connection. It's important to address these issues head-on and seek support from a therapist or counselor if needed. Ultimately, maintaining a spiritual connection in a marriage requires effort, patience, and a willingness to grow and evolve together. By facing these common challenges head-on and making your relationship a priority, you can strengthen your spiritual connection and create a deeper, more fulfilling partnership.

Marriage and Faith: Finding Spiritual Connection in Your Relationship

Marriage and Faith: Finding Spiritual Connection in Your Relationship

02

Chapter 2: Navigating Marriage Counseling with a Faith-Based Approach

How Faith Can Enhance the Effectiveness of Marriage Counseling

Marriage counseling can be a powerful tool for couples struggling to navigate the challenges of married life. However, for those who share a strong faith, incorporating their beliefs into the counseling process can significantly enhance its effectiveness. Faith can provide couples with a framework for understanding their relationship and the struggles they face. It can offer them a sense of purpose and meaning, guiding them towards forgiveness, compassion, and patience. By grounding their counseling sessions in their faith, couples can tap into a source of strength and resilience that can help them weather even the toughest storms.

Interracial couples may find that their faith helps them bridge cultural differences and navigate societal pressures. Couples dealing with financial strain can turn to their faith for guidance on managing money and finding contentment in simplicity. Those grappling with mental health issues can find solace in their beliefs, knowing that they are not alone in their struggles.

Parents can draw on their faith to guide them in raising their children with love, patience, and understanding. Couples dealing with infidelity can turn to their faith for forgiveness and healing. Communication barriers can be broken down by a shared spiritual connection, allowing couples to truly listen to and understand each other. No matter what challenges a couple may be facing, faith can provide them with a solid foundation on which to build a strong and lasting relationship. By incorporating their beliefs into their marriage counseling, couples can deepen their connection, find renewed strength, and create a more fulfilling partnership.

Finding a Counselor Who Incorporates Faith into Therapy

Finding a counselor who incorporates faith into therapy can be a valuable resource for couples looking to strengthen their spiritual connection and navigate the challenges of marriage. When seeking a counselor who integrates faith into their practice, it is important to consider a few key factors.

Marriage and Faith: Finding Spiritual Connection in Your Relationship

First and foremost, it is essential to find a counselor who aligns with your religious beliefs and values. This will ensure that the counseling sessions are meaningful and effective in addressing your unique spiritual needs. It is also important to inquire about the counselor's training and experience in incorporating faith into therapy. A counselor who has a background in religious studies or has received specialized training in faith-based counseling will be better equipped to address your spiritual concerns. Additionally, it is important to discuss with the counselor how they incorporate faith into therapy and what their approach will look like. Some counselors may use scripture, prayer, or other religious practices as part of the therapy process, while others may simply integrate spiritual principles into their counseling sessions. It is important to communicate your preferences and expectations with the counselor to ensure that you are comfortable with their approach.

Ultimately, finding a counselor who incorporates faith into therapy can be a powerful tool for couples looking to deepen their spiritual connection and strengthen their relationship. By considering the counselor's religious beliefs, training, and approach to integrating faith into therapy, couples can find a counselor who is well-suited to address their spiritual and relational needs.

Integrating Faith into Couples Therapy Sessions

Integrating faith into couples therapy sessions can be a powerful tool for strengthening the spiritual connection in your relationship. By incorporating your beliefs and values into your therapy sessions, you can deepen your understanding of each other and create a stronger bond based on shared faith.

One way to integrate faith into couples therapy is to begin each session with a prayer or meditation. This can help set the tone for the session and create a sense of spiritual connection between you and your partner. You can also incorporate scripture readings or spiritual teachings into your discussions, using them as a guide for navigating challenges in your relationship.

Another way to integrate faith into therapy is to explore how your beliefs impact your relationship dynamics. For example, if you both come from different religious backgrounds, you may need to work through how to navigate those differences in a way that honors both of your faith traditions. By exploring these issues in therapy, you can gain a deeper understanding of how your beliefs shape your relationship and learn how to support each other in your spiritual journeys.

Integrating faith into couples therapy can also be a source of strength and support during difficult times. By turning to your faith for guidance and comfort, you can find the strength to navigate challenges in your relationship and grow closer as a couple. Ultimately, integrating faith into therapy can help you build a relationship that is grounded in love, trust, and spiritual connection.

03

Chapter 3:
Embracing Diversity
in Interracial
Marriages

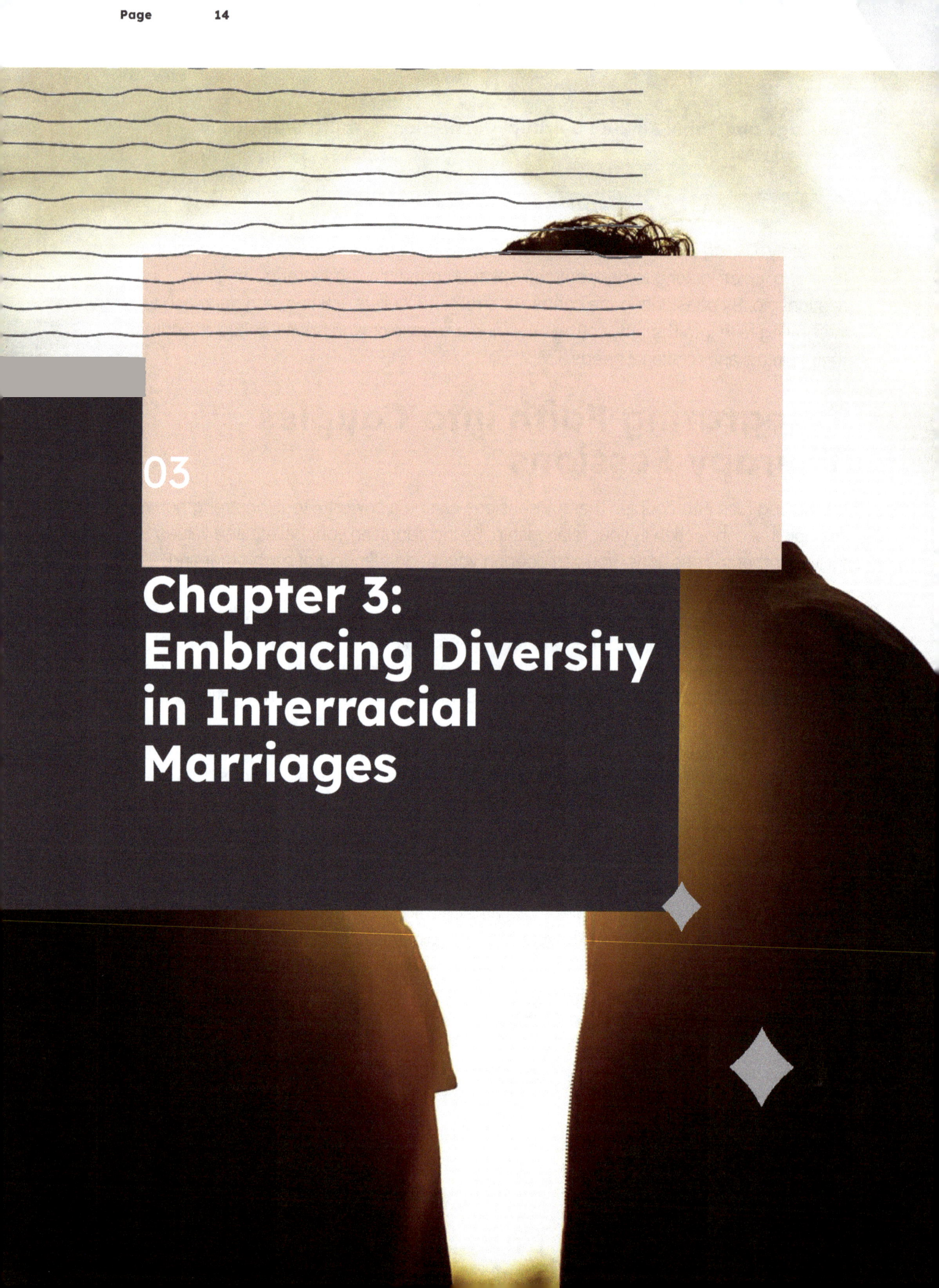

Celebrating Differences in Interracial Relationships

Interracial relationships are becoming increasingly common in today's society, yet they still face unique challenges that can strain the relationship. However, celebrating the differences in interracial relationships can actually strengthen the bond between partners and create a more fulfilling and enriching connection.

One of the key aspects of celebrating differences in interracial relationships is embracing each other's cultural backgrounds. Learning about and participating in each other's traditions, customs, and beliefs can help partners gain a deeper understanding and appreciation for one another. This can lead to a stronger sense of unity and connection, as well as a more enriched and diverse family life.

Communication is also essential in celebrating differences in interracial relationships. Open and honest conversations about race, ethnicity, and cultural differences can help partners navigate any conflicts or misunderstandings that may arise. It is important for both partners to listen and validate each other's experiences, feelings, and perspectives in order to foster a sense of mutual respect and understanding.

Furthermore, celebrating differences in interracial relationships can also help break down stereotypes and promote diversity and inclusion within the relationship and the broader community. By embracing and celebrating each other's differences, partners can serve as positive role models for others and help promote a more inclusive and accepting society.

In conclusion, celebrating differences in interracial relationships can lead to a more harmonious, fulfilling, and spiritually connected partnership. By embracing each other's cultural backgrounds, communicating openly and honestly, and promoting diversity and inclusion, partners can create a strong and resilient bond that transcends race, ethnicity, and cultural differences.

Overcoming Challenges Unique to Interracial Marriages

Interracial marriages come with their own set of challenges that can test the strength of a relationship. In this subchapter, we will explore some of the unique obstacles that couples in interracial marriages may face and provide strategies for overcoming them.

One of the biggest challenges in interracial marriages is dealing with societal attitudes and prejudices. Some people may not understand or approve of your relationship, which can lead to feelings of isolation and discrimination. It is important for couples to have open and honest conversations about these issues and support each other in the face of adversity.

Another challenge that often arises in interracial marriages is navigating different cultural backgrounds and traditions. It is essential for couples to respect and appreciate each other's cultural heritage while also finding common ground and creating new traditions together. This can require patience, compromise, and a willingness to learn from each other.

Communication is key in any marriage, but it is especially important in interracial relationships where misunderstandings can easily arise due to cultural differences. Couples should make an effort to listen actively, ask questions, and clarify any assumptions to ensure that they are on the same page.

Ultimately, overcoming the challenges unique to interracial marriages requires a strong foundation of love, trust, and mutual respect. Couples should lean on each other for support, seek guidance from trusted mentors or therapists, and continue to strengthen their spiritual connection to weather any storms that may come their way. By facing these challenges head-on and working together as a team, couples in interracial marriages can build a strong and resilient relationship that stands the test of time.

Cultivating a Strong Spiritual Bond in a Multicultural Marriage

In today's diverse and interconnected world, multicultural marriages are becoming more common. These relationships can be incredibly enriching, but they also come with their own set of challenges. One of the key aspects of a successful multicultural marriage is the cultivation of a strong spiritual bond between partners.

Marriage and Faith: Finding Spiritual Connection in Your Relationship

In a multicultural marriage, both partners bring their own unique cultural and religious backgrounds to the relationship. This can sometimes lead to differences in beliefs, values, and practices that may create tension or conflict. However, by actively working to cultivate a strong spiritual bond, couples can navigate these differences and create a strong foundation for their relationship.

One way to cultivate a strong spiritual bond in a multicultural marriage is to engage in open and honest communication about your beliefs and values. This means actively listening to your partner's perspective, respecting their beliefs, and finding common ground where possible. By creating a space for open dialogue, you can deepen your understanding of each other's spiritual beliefs and create a sense of unity in your relationship.

Another important aspect of cultivating a strong spiritual bond is to actively engage in spiritual practices together. This could involve attending religious services together, participating in spiritual rituals, or simply setting aside time for prayer or meditation as a couple. By sharing these experiences, you can create a sense of closeness and connection that transcends cultural and religious differences.

Marriage and Faith: Finding Spiritual Connection in Your Relationship

Ultimately, cultivating a strong spiritual bond in a multicultural marriage requires patience, understanding, and a willingness to learn from each other. By actively working to bridge the gap between your cultural and religious differences, you can create a relationship that is truly built on love, respect, and spiritual connection.

04

Chapter 4: Managing Finances as a Team in Marriage

The Impact of Financial Stress on Marriage

Financial stress is one of the leading causes of conflict in marriages today. The impact of financial stress on a marriage can be significant, affecting not only the couple's financial well-being but also their emotional and physical health.

When a couple is under financial stress, it can lead to arguments, resentment, and a breakdown in communication. The pressure of not being able to pay bills or provide for a family can cause feelings of inadequacy, shame, and fear. This can result in one or both partners withdrawing emotionally, leading to a lack of intimacy and connection in the relationship.

Financial stress can also exacerbate existing issues in a marriage, such as differences in spending habits, saving priorities, or financial goals. It can highlight power imbalances in the relationship, as one partner may feel more burdened or responsible for the financial situation. Moreover, financial stress can impact mental health, leading to anxiety, depression, and other emotional issues. This can further strain the marriage, as one or both partners may struggle to cope with the added pressure and uncertainty.

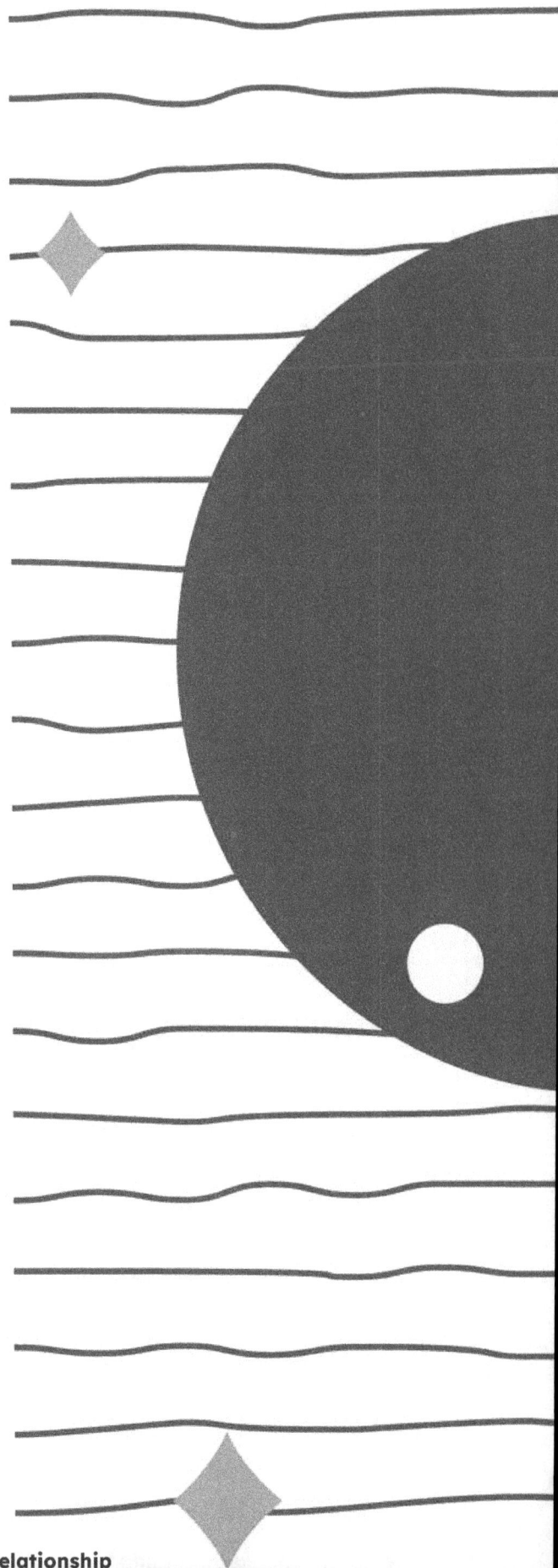

In order to address the impact of financial stress on marriage, it is important for couples to communicate openly and honestly about their financial situation. This includes discussing their fears, anxieties, and goals related to money. Seeking professional help from a marriage counselor or financial advisor can also be beneficial in navigating financial challenges and finding solutions that work for both partners.

By acknowledging the impact of financial stress on their marriage and working together to address it, couples can strengthen their bond, build resilience, and find a deeper spiritual connection in their relationship.

Budgeting and Financial Planning Strategies for Couples

Budgeting and financial planning are crucial aspects of any relationship, especially for couples who are looking to build a strong foundation for their future together. Money can often be a source of tension and conflict in a marriage, but with the right strategies in place, it can also be a tool for building trust, communication, and unity.

One of the first steps in creating a budgeting and financial planning strategy for couples is to have open and honest conversations about money. This includes discussing individual spending habits, financial goals, and any debts or financial obligations that each partner may have. By having these conversations early on in the relationship, couples can establish a sense of transparency and trust when it comes to their finances.

Another important aspect of budgeting and financial planning for couples is setting shared financial goals. This could include saving for a down payment on a house, planning for children's education, or setting aside funds for retirement. By working together to achieve these goals, couples can build a sense of teamwork and collaboration when it comes to their finances.

It's also important for couples to establish a budget that works for both partners. This may involve creating a joint bank account for shared expenses, setting spending limits for discretionary purchases, and tracking expenses to ensure that both partners are on the same page when it comes to their finances.

By implementing these budgeting and financial planning strategies, couples can create a solid foundation for their relationship and build a sense of financial security for the future. Communication, trust, and teamwork are key components of successful budgeting and financial planning for couples, and by working together, couples can achieve their financial goals and strengthen their relationship in the process.

Using Faith to Guide Financial Decision Making in Marriage

Money is often cited as one of the top reasons for conflict in marriages. Finances can be a source of stress and tension, but they can also be an opportunity for growth and unity in a marriage. When couples use faith to guide their financial decision making, they can strengthen their relationship and build a solid foundation for their future together.

Marriage and Faith: Finding Spiritual Connection in Your Relationship

One of the key principles of using faith to guide financial decision making in marriage is trust. Trusting in a higher power can help couples let go of their fears and anxieties about money, knowing that they are being guided and supported in their financial journey. This trust can also help couples communicate openly and honestly about their financial goals and priorities, creating a sense of unity and shared purpose.

Another important aspect of using faith in financial decision making is gratitude. By recognizing the blessings and abundance in their lives, couples can cultivate a spirit of generosity and giving, both towards each other and towards those in need. This attitude of gratitude can help couples appreciate the value of money and resources, leading to more mindful and intentional financial decisions.

Finally, faith can provide couples with a sense of perspective and purpose when it comes to money. By aligning their financial goals with their values and beliefs, couples can make decisions that are in line with their spiritual principles, leading to a more fulfilling and meaningful life together.

Overall, using faith to guide financial decision making in marriage can help couples navigate the challenges and opportunities that come with managing money in a relationship. By trusting in a higher power, practicing gratitude, and aligning their financial decisions with their values, couples can build a strong and resilient partnership that is grounded in love, trust, and faith.

Marriage and Faith: Finding Spiritual Connection in Your Relationship

05

Chapter 5: Nurturing Mental Health in Your Marriage

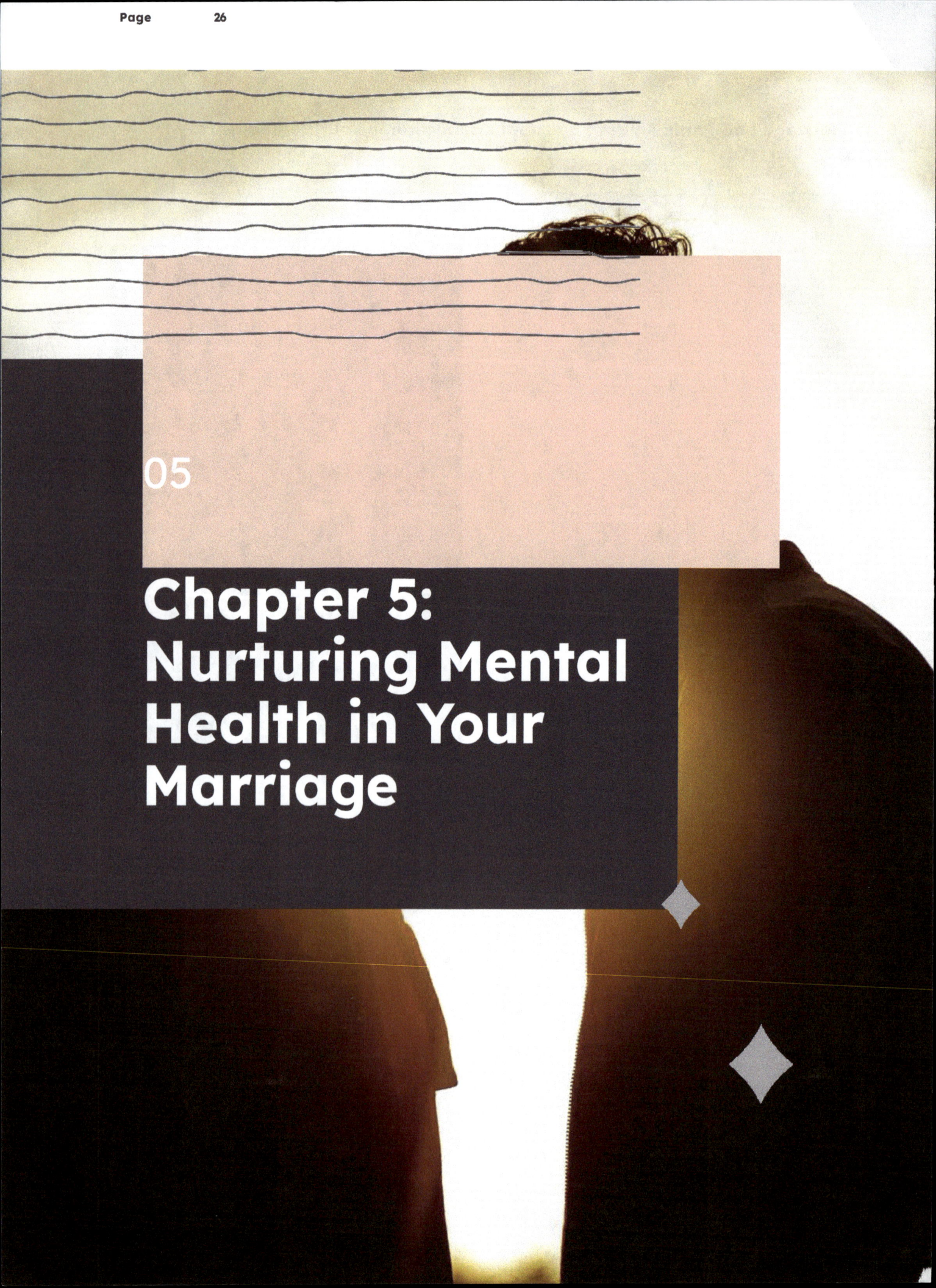

Recognizing the Signs of Mental Health Issues in Your Spouse

In any marriage, it is important to be attuned to the mental health of your partner. Mental health issues can have a significant impact on the dynamics of a relationship, and it is crucial to be able to recognize the signs and address them in a supportive and loving manner. Here are some key signs to look out for in your spouse:

1. Changes in Behavior: One of the most common signs of mental health issues is a noticeable change in behavior. This can manifest in various ways, such as increased irritability, mood swings, withdrawal from social activities, or even reckless behavior.

2. Physical Symptoms: Mental health issues can also manifest in physical symptoms, such as headaches, stomach problems, or unexplained aches and pains. If your spouse is experiencing these symptoms without any clear medical cause, it could be a sign of underlying mental health issues.

3. Changes in Sleep Patterns: Disrupted sleep patterns, such as insomnia or oversleeping, can be indicative of mental health issues. Pay attention to any changes in your spouse's sleep habits and consider discussing them with a mental health professional.

4. Loss of Interest: A loss of interest in activities that your spouse once enjoyed can be a red flag for mental health issues. If they seem disengaged or apathetic towards things they used to love, it may be time to seek help.

5. Difficulty Concentrating: Mental health issues can also impact cognitive function, leading to difficulty concentrating, making decisions, or remembering things. If your spouse is struggling in these areas, it could be a sign of a larger issue.

In conclusion, recognizing the signs of mental health issues in your spouse is essential for maintaining a healthy and supportive relationship. By being attentive to changes in behavior, physical symptoms, sleep patterns, loss of interest, and cognitive function, you can better understand and address any mental health challenges your spouse may be facing. Remember, seeking help from a mental health professional is always a wise decision when it comes to supporting your spouse through difficult times.

Seeking Professional Help with a Faith-Based Approach

Marriage and Faith: Finding Spiritual Connection in Your Relationship

When facing challenges in your marriage, it can be beneficial to seek professional help from a counselor or therapist with a faith-based approach. These professionals can provide guidance and support based on your religious beliefs and values, helping you and your partner strengthen your spiritual connection and find solutions to your relationship issues.

Marriage counseling with a faith-based approach can be particularly helpful for couples who share a common religious background or who value spirituality in their lives. By incorporating your faith into the counseling process, you can explore how your beliefs and values impact your relationship and work together to deepen your spiritual connection.

Interracial couples may also benefit from seeking counseling with a faith-based approach, as it can help them navigate the unique challenges they may face due to cultural differences and societal pressures. A counselor who understands and respects the diversity of your relationship can provide valuable insight and support as you work to build a strong and united front.

In addition to addressing common marriage issues such as finances, mental health, parenting, infidelity, communication, and career challenges, a faith-based approach to counseling can also help couples explore the role of religion and spirituality in their relationship. By examining how your beliefs shape your views on marriage and love, you can gain a deeper understanding of each other and strengthen your bond.

Whether you are struggling with conflicts in your marriage or simply want to enhance your spiritual connection, seeking professional help with a faith-based approach can provide you with the guidance and support you need to build a strong and fulfilling relationship. By incorporating your faith into the counseling process, you can work together with your partner to overcome obstacles and grow closer in your journey towards a lasting and meaningful partnership.

Supporting Each Other's Mental Health Journey

Supporting each other's mental health journey in a marriage is crucial for maintaining a strong and healthy relationship. Mental health issues can affect not only the individual but also the dynamics of the marriage itself. It is important for couples to recognize the signs of mental health struggles in each other and offer support and understanding. Communication is key when it comes to supporting each other's mental health journey. It is important for couples to have open and honest conversations about how they are feeling and what they need from each other. This can help create a safe space for both partners to express their emotions and concerns without judgment.

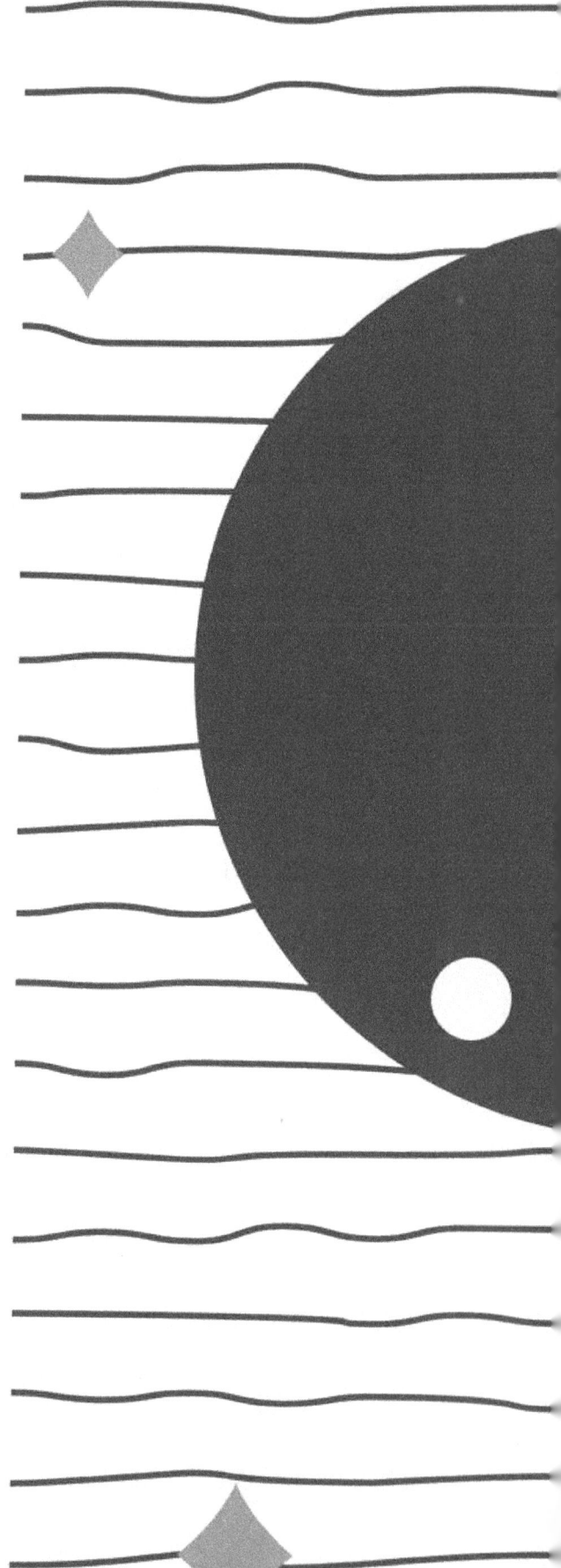

Marriage and Faith: Finding Spiritual Connection in Your Relationship

Another important aspect of supporting each other's mental health journey is being there for each other during difficult times. This may involve offering a listening ear, providing emotional support, or even seeking professional help together. It is important for couples to show empathy and compassion towards each other's struggles and to work together towards finding solutions.

Additionally, couples can support each other's mental health journey by taking care of themselves as well. This may involve practicing self-care, seeking therapy or counseling, or engaging in activities that promote mental well-being. By taking care of themselves, couples can better support each other and strengthen their relationship.

Overall, supporting each other's mental health journey in a marriage requires patience, understanding, and a willingness to work together towards a common goal. By prioritizing mental health and offering support to each other, couples can create a strong foundation for a healthy and fulfilling relationship.

06

Chapter 6: Co-Parenting with a Unified Spiritual Foundation

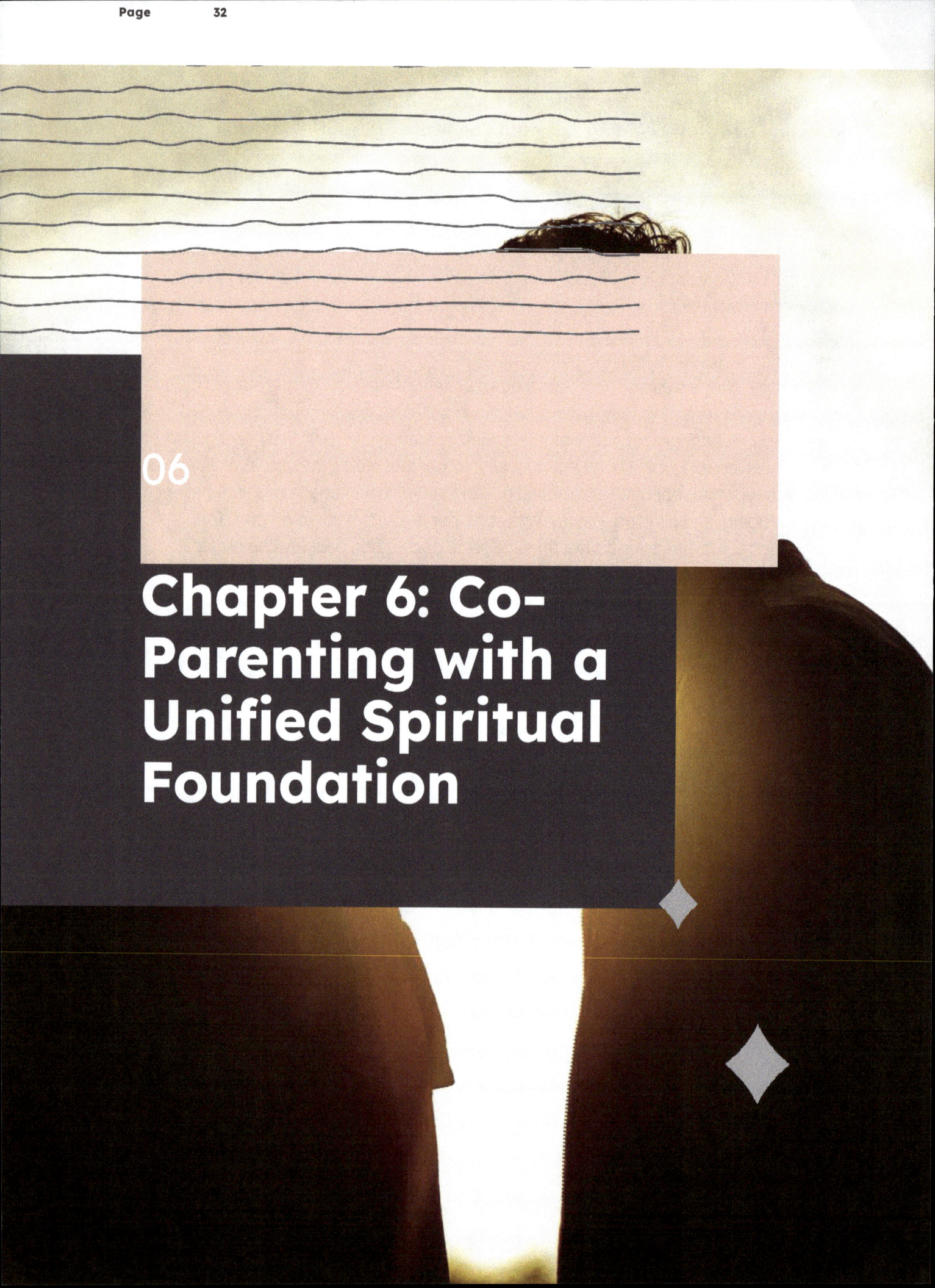

Instilling Values and Beliefs in Your Children

Instilling values and beliefs in your children is a crucial aspect of parenting that can greatly impact their development and future relationships. As parents, it is our responsibility to guide our children in understanding right from wrong, and to help them develop a strong moral compass that will serve them well throughout their lives.

One of the most effective ways to instill values and beliefs in your children is by leading by example. Children learn by observing the behavior of their parents, so it is important to demonstrate the values and beliefs that you wish to instill in them. This means being honest, respectful, and compassionate in your interactions with others, and showing your children what it means to live a life guided by strong principles.

Communication is also key when it comes to instilling values and beliefs in your children. Take the time to have open and honest conversations with them about important topics such as honesty, kindness, and empathy. Encourage them to ask questions and share their thoughts and feelings, and listen to what they have to say without judgment.

It is also important to create a supportive and nurturing environment in which your children feel safe to express themselves and explore their own beliefs and values. Encourage them to think critically about the world around them, and to question what they see and hear. By fostering a sense of curiosity and openness in your children, you can help them develop a strong sense of self and a deep understanding of their own values and beliefs.

Overall, instilling values and beliefs in your children is a lifelong process that requires patience, consistency, and love. By leading by example, communicating openly and honestly, and creating a supportive environment, you can help your children develop the moral foundation they need to navigate the complexities of the world and build strong, healthy relationships in the future.

Balancing Parenting Styles with Faith

When it comes to raising children, couples often find themselves facing challenges in balancing their different parenting styles with their faith. This can lead to conflicts and disagreements that may strain the relationship if not addressed effectively. In this subchapter, we will explore how couples can navigate this delicate balance and find harmony in their approach to parenting while staying true to their beliefs.

One of the first steps in balancing parenting styles with faith is to have open and honest communication with your partner. Discuss your beliefs, values, and expectations when it comes to raising children, and try to find common ground where you can both compromise and support each other. It is important to respect each other's perspectives and find ways to incorporate both of your beliefs into your parenting approach.

Another important aspect to consider is the impact of your faith on your parenting decisions. Your religious beliefs can greatly influence how you choose to raise your children, from the values you instill in them to the discipline methods you use. It is important to be mindful of how your faith guides your parenting style and to ensure that it aligns with your partner's beliefs as well.

Seeking guidance from a trusted spiritual advisor or counselor can also be beneficial in navigating the challenges of balancing parenting styles with faith. They can provide valuable insights and support as you work through any conflicts or disagreements that may arise.

By being mindful of each other's beliefs, values, and parenting styles, couples can find a way to raise their children in a way that honors their faith while also fostering a strong and loving relationship. Balancing parenting styles with faith may require compromise and understanding, but with patience and communication, couples can create a harmonious and spiritually connected approach to raising their children.

Strengthening Your Marriage Through Co-Parenting

Marriage and Faith: Finding Spiritual Connection in Your Relationship

Co-parenting can be a challenging yet rewarding aspect of marriage. It involves both partners working together to raise their children in a loving and supportive environment. While it may seem like a daunting task, co-parenting can actually strengthen your marriage and deepen your bond as a couple.

One key aspect of successful co-parenting is communication. It is important for both partners to be on the same page when it comes to parenting decisions. This means discussing discipline strategies, setting boundaries, and creating a united front when it comes to making important decisions for your children. By communicating openly and honestly with each other, you can avoid misunderstandings and conflicts that can strain your marriage.

Another important aspect of co-parenting is teamwork. It is essential for both partners to work together as a team when it comes to parenting their children. This means dividing responsibilities, supporting each other, and making decisions together. By working as a team, you can create a strong foundation for your marriage and provide a stable and loving environment for your children.

It is also important to prioritize your marriage while co-parenting. It can be easy to get caught up in the demands of parenting and forget to nurture your relationship with your partner. Make time for each other, go on dates, and communicate openly about your feelings and needs. By prioritizing your marriage, you can strengthen your bond as a couple and set a positive example for your children.

Marriage and Faith: Finding Spiritual Connection in Your Relationship

In conclusion, co-parenting can be a challenging yet rewarding aspect of marriage. By communicating effectively, working as a team, and prioritizing your marriage, you can strengthen your relationship and create a loving and supportive environment for your children. Remember that you are a team, and by working together, you can overcome any obstacles that come your way.

Marriage and Faith: Finding Spiritual Connection in Your Relationship

07

Chapter 7: Healing from the Pain of Infidelity with Faith

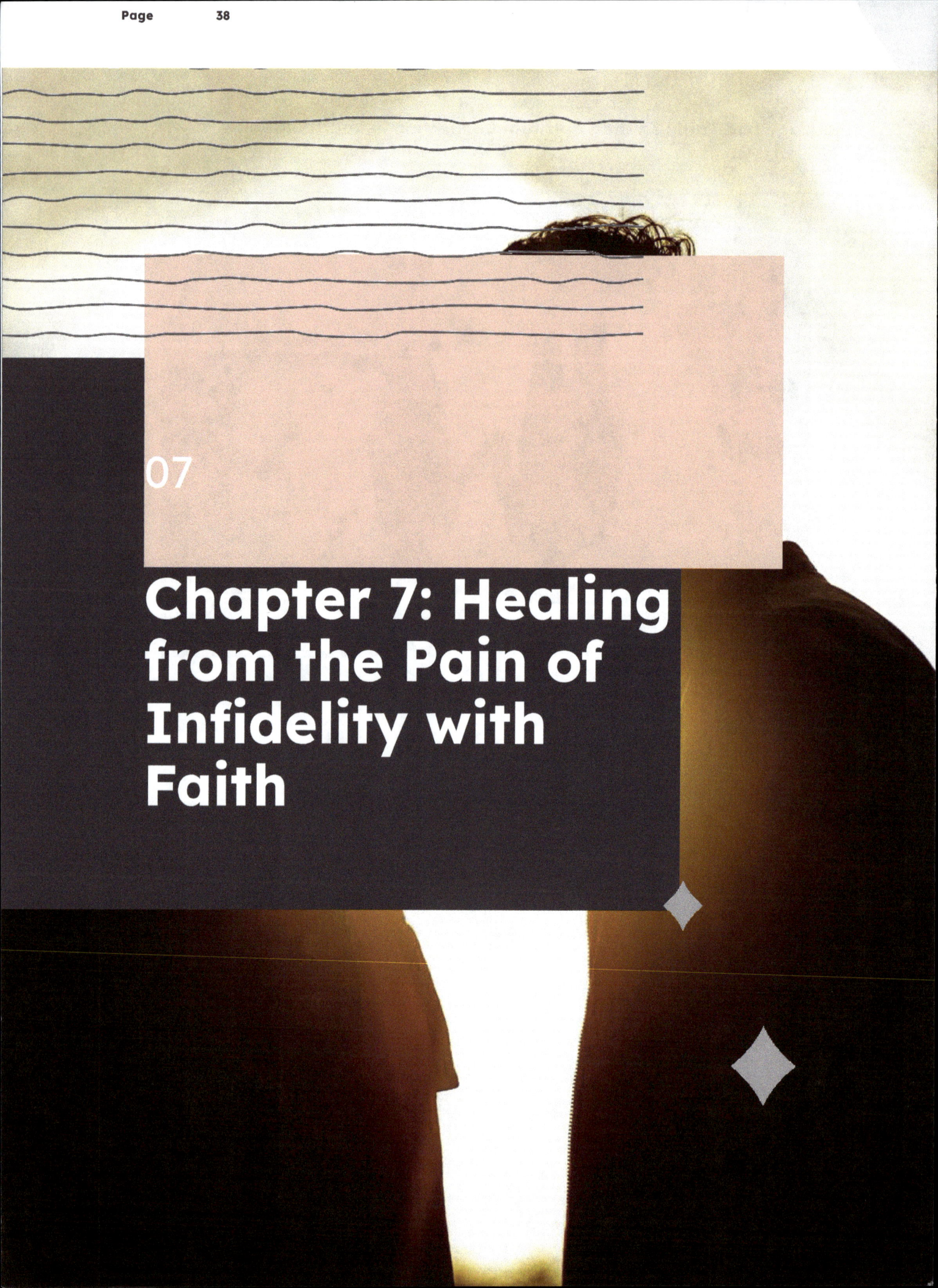

Rebuilding Trust and Forgiveness in a Marriage

Rebuilding trust and forgiveness in a marriage is a crucial step towards healing and strengthening the bond between partners. Trust is the foundation of any successful relationship, and when it is broken, it can be challenging to repair. However, with patience, understanding, and a commitment to forgiveness, couples can work through their issues and rebuild the trust that was lost.

One of the first steps towards rebuilding trust is open and honest communication. Both partners need to be willing to share their thoughts and feelings, even if it is uncomfortable or difficult. This can help to create a safe space for both individuals to express themselves and work through any lingering issues.

Forgiveness is also a key component of rebuilding trust. It is important to remember that forgiveness is not about condoning the actions that caused the hurt, but rather about letting go of the anger and resentment that can hold a couple back from moving forward. Forgiveness can be a powerful tool in healing a relationship and allowing both partners to move on from past mistakes.

In addition to communication and forgiveness, couples may also benefit from seeking outside help, such as marriage counseling. A trained therapist can provide guidance and support as couples navigate the challenges of rebuilding trust and forgiveness in their marriage.

Ultimately, rebuilding trust and forgiveness in a marriage requires patience, understanding, and a willingness to work through difficult emotions. By committing to open communication, forgiveness, and seeking outside help when needed, couples can strengthen their bond and create a solid foundation for a healthy and fulfilling relationship.

Seeking Guidance from Spiritual Leaders or Counselors

In times of trouble or uncertainty in your marriage, turning to spiritual leaders or counselors can be a valuable source of support and guidance. These individuals are often trained in helping couples navigate the complexities of relationships and can provide a fresh perspective on your situation.

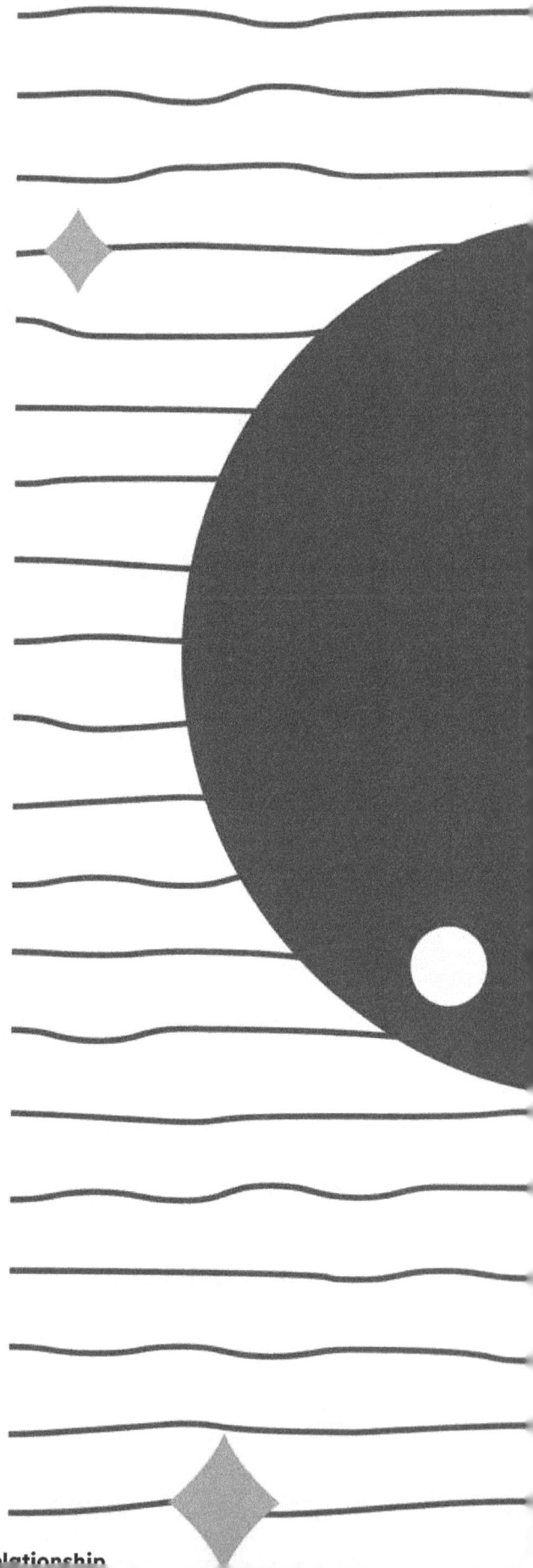

Marriage and Faith: Finding Spiritual Connection in Your Relationship

Whether you are struggling with communication issues, financial stress, infidelity, or any other challenge in your marriage, seeking guidance from a spiritual leader or counselor can help you and your partner gain clarity and find solutions to your problems. They can offer a safe space for you to discuss your feelings, fears, and desires openly and honestly. Interracial couples may face unique challenges in their marriage, and seeking guidance from a spiritual leader or counselor who understands these dynamics can be especially helpful. They can help you navigate any cultural differences or prejudices that may arise and assist you in building a strong and resilient relationship.

For couples dealing with mental health issues, parenting struggles, or long-distance relationships, a spiritual leader or counselor can offer valuable insights and strategies for overcoming these obstacles. They can help you and your partner develop healthy coping mechanisms and communication skills to strengthen your bond and overcome any challenges you may face.

No matter what issues you are facing in your marriage, seeking guidance from a spiritual leader or counselor can provide you with the support and tools you need to navigate these challenges and strengthen your relationship. Remember, you do not have to face these difficulties alone – reach out for help and support when you need it.

Moving Forward with Faith and Hope

In the journey of marriage, there are bound to be challenges that test the strength of your relationship. When faced with obstacles, it is essential to move forward with faith and hope. This subchapter explores how faith and hope can be powerful tools in navigating the ups and downs of married life.

Having faith in your partner and in the strength of your relationship can help you weather any storm. Trusting that you are both committed to working through issues together can provide a sense of security and stability. This faith can also extend to a higher power, providing a sense of divine guidance and support in times of need.

Hope is another crucial element in moving forward in marriage. It is the belief that better days are ahead and that with effort and dedication, you can overcome any challenges that come your way. Keeping a positive outlook and focusing on the possibilities for growth and healing can help you stay motivated and optimistic about the future of your relationship.

Incorporating faith and hope into your marriage can also strengthen your spiritual connection. By relying on your shared beliefs and values, you can find a deeper sense of purpose and meaning in your relationship. This spiritual bond can provide a strong foundation for facing any obstacles that may arise.

Ultimately, moving forward with faith and hope requires a willingness to be open and vulnerable with your partner. By communicating openly and honestly about your fears, hopes, and dreams, you can create a sense of unity and trust that will carry you through even the toughest times. With faith and hope as your guiding lights, you can navigate the challenges of marriage with grace and resilience.

08

Chapter 8: Enhancing Communication Through Spiritual Connection

The Role of Active Listening in a Spiritual Marriage

In the journey of a spiritual marriage, active listening plays a crucial role in fostering understanding, empathy, and connection between partners. Active listening involves not just hearing words, but truly listening to the emotions and intentions behind them. It requires giving your full attention to your partner, without judgment or interruption.

In a spiritual marriage, active listening is a way of showing love and respect for your partner's thoughts and feelings. By truly listening to your partner, you are creating a safe space for them to express themselves fully and honestly. This can lead to deeper emotional intimacy and strengthen the bond between you and your spouse.

Active listening also helps in resolving conflicts and misunderstandings in a healthy way. By listening attentively to your partner's perspective, you are better able to see things from their point of view and find common ground. This can prevent arguments from escalating and promote peaceful resolutions.

Furthermore, active listening in a spiritual marriage involves being present in the moment and practicing mindfulness. It means putting aside distractions and focusing solely on your partner and the conversation at hand. This level of attentiveness can enhance communication and deepen the emotional connection between you and your spouse.

In conclusion, active listening is a powerful tool in nurturing a spiritual marriage. By practicing this skill regularly, couples can improve their communication, strengthen their emotional bond, and create a deeper sense of unity and understanding in their relationship. So, take the time to truly listen to your partner with an open heart and mind, and watch as your marriage blossoms into a beautiful and fulfilling spiritual union.

Using Prayer and Meditation to Improve Communication

Marriage and Faith: Finding Spiritual Connection in Your Relationship

In any relationship, communication is key. It forms the foundation of a strong and healthy partnership. However, sometimes, communication can break down, leading to misunderstandings, arguments, and resentment. In these moments, turning to prayer and meditation can be a powerful tool to improve communication and strengthen your bond with your partner.

Prayer is a way to connect with a higher power and seek guidance and support in your relationship. By praying together, you can create a sense of unity and shared purpose. It can help you both to express your hopes, fears, and desires, as well as ask for help in resolving conflicts or finding common ground. Taking the time to pray together can also foster a sense of intimacy and trust, deepening your emotional connection.

Meditation, on the other hand, can help you to calm your mind and focus on the present moment. By practicing mindfulness, you can become more aware of your thoughts, emotions, and reactions, allowing you to communicate more effectively with your partner. Meditation can also help you to let go of negative emotions and cultivate a sense of compassion and empathy towards your partner.

By incorporating prayer and meditation into your daily routine, you can create a sacred space for open and honest communication with your partner. It can help you to listen more attentively, speak more thoughtfully, and resolve conflicts more peacefully. Ultimately, by using prayer and meditation to improve communication, you can build a stronger, more resilient relationship based on love, understanding, and faith.

Resolving Conflict with a Faith-Based Approach

In any relationship, conflict is inevitable. Whether it's about finances, career choices, parenting styles, or any other issue, disagreements will arise. However, resolving these conflicts in a healthy and productive manner is key to maintaining a strong and successful relationship.

One approach to resolving conflict that many couples find helpful is a faith-based approach. This involves turning to your spiritual beliefs and values to guide you through difficult times and help you find common ground with your partner.

One of the first steps in using a faith-based approach to resolve conflict is to pray together. Taking the time to pray as a couple can help you both gain perspective and clarity on the issue at hand. It can also help you both feel more connected to each other and to a higher power, which can bring a sense of peace and understanding to the situation. Another important aspect of a faith-based approach to conflict resolution is forgiveness. In any relationship, forgiveness is essential for moving forward and healing past wounds. By turning to your faith and seeking guidance from your spiritual beliefs, you can find the strength to forgive your partner and let go of any resentment or anger.

Finally, a faith-based approach to conflict resolution involves seeking guidance from your religious or spiritual leader. Whether it's a pastor, priest, rabbi, imam, or another religious figure, talking to someone who shares your beliefs can provide valuable insight and support as you work through your differences.

Marriage and Faith: Finding Spiritual Connection in Your Relationship

By incorporating a faith-based approach to conflict resolution into your relationship, you can strengthen your spiritual connection with your partner and find a deeper sense of understanding, compassion, and love. Through prayer, forgiveness, and seeking guidance from your faith community, you can navigate even the toughest conflicts with grace and humility.

09

Chapter 9: Balancing Career and Marriage with Faith

Setting Priorities and Boundaries in Your Career

Setting priorities and boundaries in your career is crucial for maintaining a healthy work-life balance, especially in the context of a marriage or relationship. In today's fast-paced world, it can be easy to get caught up in the demands of your job and neglect the needs of your partner or family. However, by setting clear priorities and boundaries, you can ensure that your career does not overshadow your personal relationships. One key aspect of setting priorities in your career is identifying what truly matters to you. Take the time to reflect on your values and goals, both in your professional and personal life. By understanding what is most important to you, you can make informed decisions about where to focus your time and energy. This may involve making sacrifices or tough choices, but ultimately it will help you align your career with your values and priorities.

Additionally, setting boundaries in your career is essential for maintaining a healthy work-life balance. This means establishing clear limits on the time and energy you are willing to devote to work, and communicating these boundaries to your employer and colleagues. It also involves setting boundaries around technology use, such as limiting the amount of time you spend checking emails or taking work calls outside of office hours.

By setting priorities and boundaries in your career, you can create space for your relationship to thrive. This may involve making compromises and finding creative solutions to balance your professional and personal responsibilities. Remember, your career is just one aspect of your life, and it should not come at the expense of your relationship or family. Prioritize what truly matters to you, and set boundaries to protect your time and energy for those you love.

Supporting Each Other's Career Goals with Faith

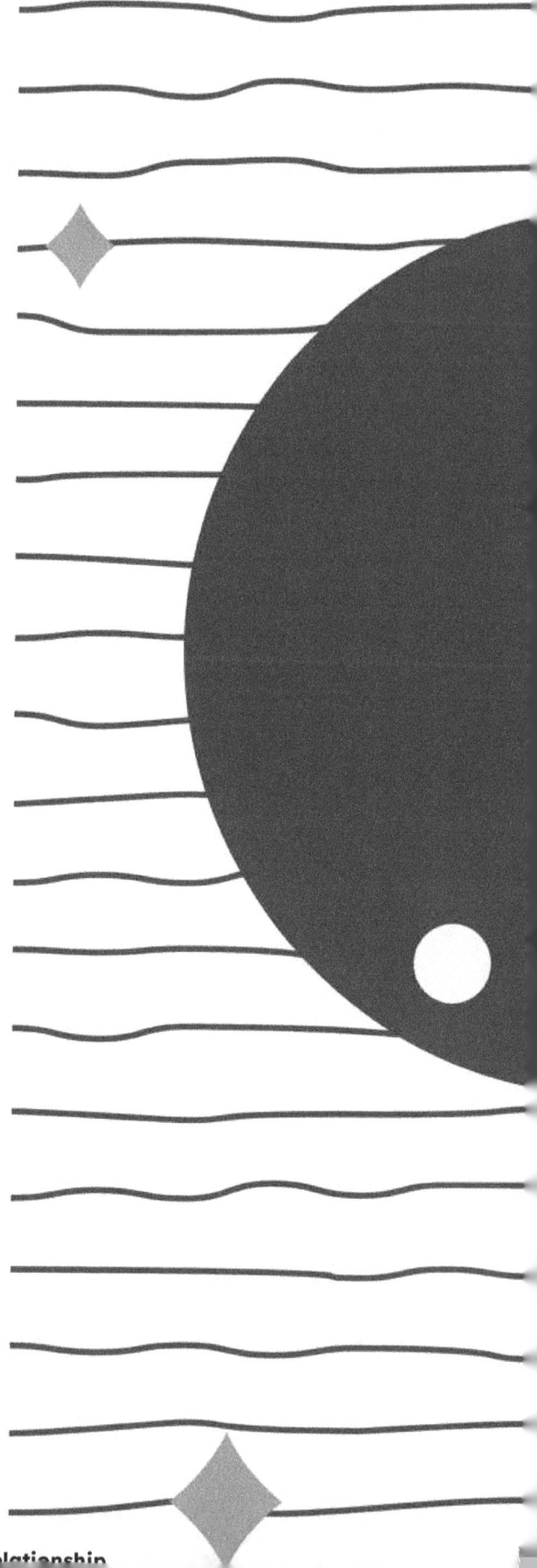

Marriage and Faith: Finding Spiritual Connection in Your Relationship

Supporting each other's career goals with faith is a key aspect of building a strong and successful marriage. In a relationship, it's important to not only have faith in each other but also in each other's abilities and dreams. By supporting your partner's career goals, you are showing them that you believe in their potential and are committed to helping them achieve their aspirations.

One way to support each other's career goals is through open communication. Take the time to talk to your partner about their career ambitions, what they need from you in terms of support, and how you can help them reach their goals. By having open and honest conversations about your career aspirations, you can better understand each other's needs and work together to achieve them.

Another way to support each other's career goals with faith is through encouragement and motivation. Be your partner's biggest cheerleader, celebrating their successes and providing them with the encouragement they need during challenging times. By being a source of support and motivation, you can help your partner stay focused and motivated on their career path.

Additionally, it's important to be willing to make sacrifices for each other's career goals. This may mean taking on more responsibilities at home while your partner focuses on their career, or being understanding when they need to work late or travel for business. By being willing to make sacrifices for each other's career goals, you are showing your commitment to each other's success and happiness.

In conclusion, supporting each other's career goals with faith is essential for building a strong and successful marriage. By communicating openly, providing encouragement and motivation, and being willing to make sacrifices, you can help each other achieve your career aspirations and strengthen your bond as a couple.

Finding Work-Life Balance Through Spiritual Practices

In today's fast-paced world, many couples struggle to find a balance between their professional lives and their personal relationships. The demands of work can often take a toll on our mental, emotional, and physical well-being, leaving little time or energy for our spouses or families. However, incorporating spiritual practices into our daily routine can help us find the harmony and peace we need to thrive in both areas of our lives.

One way to achieve this balance is by setting aside time each day for prayer, meditation, or reflection. By connecting with our spiritual beliefs and values, we can gain a sense of purpose and perspective that can help us navigate the challenges of our careers and relationships. This time of spiritual practice can also serve as a reminder of what is truly important to us, helping us prioritize our time and energy accordingly.

Another way to find work-life balance through spiritual practices is by integrating our beliefs into our daily activities. Whether it's through acts of kindness, gratitude, or mindfulness, incorporating our spiritual values into our work and personal lives can help us stay grounded and focused on what truly matters. By living authentically and in alignment with our beliefs, we can create a sense of peace and fulfillment that transcends the daily stresses and pressures we face.

Ultimately, finding work-life balance through spiritual practices is about honoring our values, nurturing our relationships, and staying true to ourselves amidst the chaos of modern life. By incorporating these practices into our daily routine, we can create a foundation of strength and resilience that allows us to thrive in both our careers and our relationships.

10

Chapter 10: Strengthening Your Relationship Through Shared Religion or Spirituality

Finding Common Ground in Your Beliefs

In any relationship, especially in a marriage, finding common ground in your beliefs can be crucial for building a strong spiritual connection. This subchapter will explore ways in which couples can navigate their differences in beliefs and come together in a harmonious way.

One of the first steps in finding common ground in your beliefs is to openly communicate with your partner about your respective faiths or spiritual beliefs. This means being honest about what you believe in, what values are important to you, and how you practice your faith. By having an open and honest dialogue, you can better understand where your partner is coming from and find areas of overlap or agreement.

It is also important to respect each other's beliefs, even if they may differ from your own. Remember that everyone is entitled to their own beliefs and opinions, and it is important to approach these differences with an open mind and a willingness to learn from each other.

Finding common ground in your beliefs may also involve compromising and finding ways to incorporate both of your beliefs into your relationship. This could mean attending religious services together, celebrating holidays from both of your faiths, or finding other ways to honor and respect each other's beliefs. Ultimately, finding common ground in your beliefs is about fostering a sense of unity and connection in your relationship. By embracing each other's beliefs, respecting each other's differences, and finding ways to incorporate both of your beliefs into your lives together, you can strengthen your spiritual connection and create a more harmonious and fulfilling marriage.

Participating in Religious or Spiritual Practices Together

Participating in religious or spiritual practices together can be a powerful way to strengthen the bond between partners in a marriage. Whether you both share the same faith or come from different religious backgrounds, engaging in spiritual activities together can deepen your connection and create a sense of unity.

Marriage and Faith: Finding Spiritual Connection in Your Relationship

For couples who share the same faith, attending religious services, praying together, and engaging in spiritual rituals can be a way to connect on a deeper level and reaffirm your commitment to each other. These shared experiences can provide a sense of comfort and support during challenging times, as well as a source of joy and celebration during happy moments.

For couples from different religious backgrounds, participating in each other's spiritual practices can be a way to show respect and understanding for your partner's beliefs. By learning about and engaging in your partner's religious traditions, you can gain a greater appreciation for their faith and create a sense of harmony and unity in your relationship.

Engaging in religious or spiritual practices together can also provide a sense of purpose and meaning in your marriage. By aligning your values and beliefs, you can create a strong foundation for your relationship and navigate life's challenges with a sense of shared purpose.

No matter what your religious or spiritual beliefs may be, finding ways to participate in these practices together can help you build a stronger, more connected relationship. Whether it's attending services, praying together, or engaging in spiritual discussions, taking the time to nurture your spiritual connection can bring you closer together and deepen your bond as a couple.

Growing Together in Faith as a Couple

Marriage and Faith: Finding Spiritual Connection in Your Relationship

In the journey of marriage, growing together in faith as a couple can be a transformative and enriching experience. Faith can serve as a strong foundation for a relationship, providing couples with a sense of purpose, shared values, and a deeper connection to each other.

One of the first steps in growing together in faith as a couple is to openly discuss and explore your individual beliefs and values. This can involve sharing your spiritual practices, attending religious services together, or engaging in meaningful conversations about your beliefs. By understanding each other's faith perspectives, you can create a space for mutual respect and support in your relationship.

Practicing faith together can also strengthen your bond as a couple. Whether it's praying together, reading spiritual texts, or participating in charitable activities, engaging in shared spiritual practices can deepen your connection and foster a sense of unity. By incorporating faith into your daily lives, you can find comfort, guidance, and solace in each other's presence.

Challenges may arise in the process of growing together in faith as a couple, especially if you come from different religious backgrounds. It's important to approach these differences with patience, respect, and open-mindedness. By embracing each other's beliefs and finding common ground, you can create a harmonious and inclusive spiritual environment within your relationship.

Marriage and Faith: Finding Spiritual Connection in Your Relationship

Ultimately, growing together in faith as a couple is a continuous journey of self-discovery, growth, and love. By nurturing your spiritual connection, you can strengthen the foundation of your relationship and navigate life's challenges with grace and resilience. Remember to lean on each other for support, communicate openly and honestly, and trust in the power of faith to guide you through your shared journey as a couple.

11

Chapter 11: Sustaining Love in a Long-Distance Marriage

Nurturing Your Connection Across Distance

In today's fast-paced world, many couples find themselves in long-distance relationships due to career opportunities, family obligations, or other circumstances. While being physically apart can be challenging, it is possible to nurture your connection across distance and maintain a strong and healthy relationship.

One of the most important aspects of nurturing your connection across distance is communication. Make an effort to communicate regularly with your partner through phone calls, video chats, text messages, and emails. Share your thoughts, feelings, and experiences with each other to keep the lines of communication open and strengthen your bond.

It is also crucial to make time for each other despite the distance. Schedule regular virtual dates, send surprise gifts or letters, and plan visits whenever possible. Making an effort to stay connected and involved in each other's lives will help maintain the emotional intimacy in your relationship.

Trust is another key component of nurturing your connection across distance. Trust your partner and be honest and transparent in your communication. Avoid jealousy and insecurity by building a foundation of trust and mutual respect in your relationship.

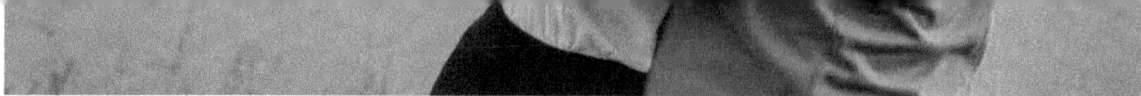

Lastly, remember to support each other's goals and dreams, even if they require you to be apart. Encourage and uplift each other, and celebrate each other's successes and achievements. By maintaining a positive and supportive attitude towards each other, you can overcome the challenges of distance and continue to grow together as a couple.

In conclusion, nurturing your connection across distance requires effort, communication, trust, and support. By prioritizing your relationship and making an active effort to stay connected, you can overcome the challenges of long-distance relationships and build a strong and lasting bond with your partner.

Using Technology to Stay Connected Spiritually

In today's fast-paced world, staying connected spiritually with your partner can sometimes be a challenge. However, with the advancements in technology, there are now more ways than ever to nurture your spiritual connection with your spouse, no matter how busy your schedules may be.

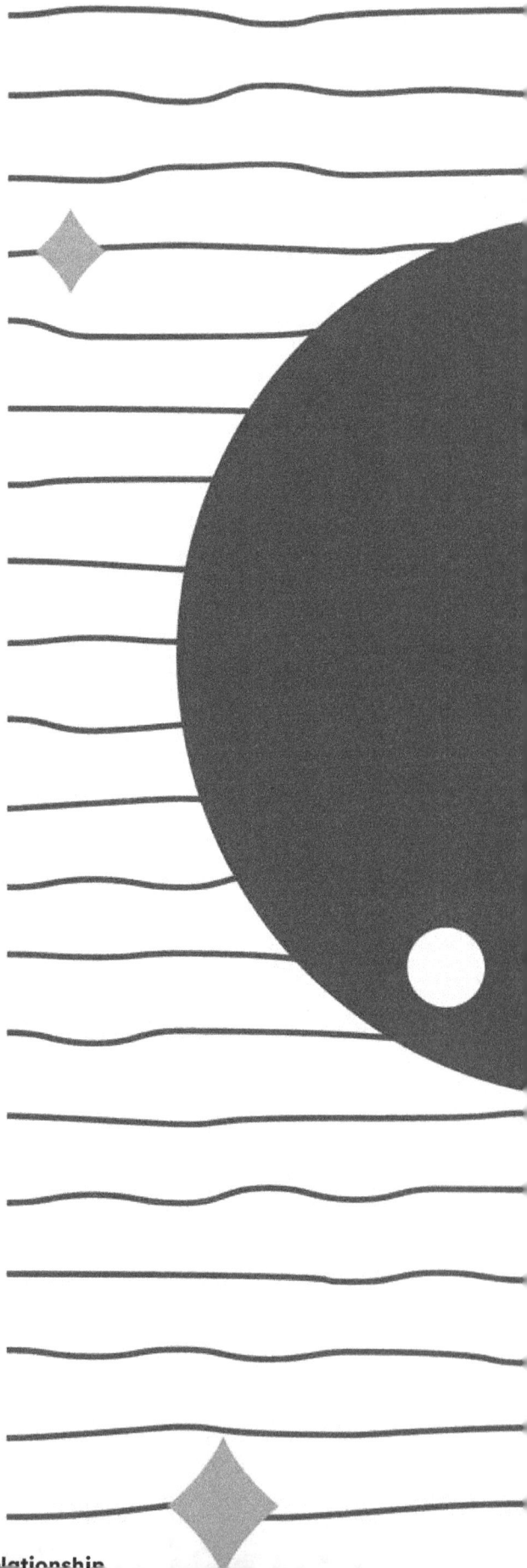

Marriage and Faith: Finding Spiritual Connection in Your Relationship

One way to use technology to stay connected spiritually is by utilizing meditation apps or online guided meditation sessions. Taking a few minutes each day to meditate together can help you both center yourselves and connect on a deeper level. Additionally, there are apps available that offer daily devotionals or spiritual readings that you can share with each other, sparking meaningful discussions and reflections.

Another way to utilize technology for spiritual connection in your marriage is by attending virtual religious services or joining online faith-based communities. Many churches and spiritual organizations now offer livestreamed services or online discussion groups, allowing you to participate in worship and engage with others who share your beliefs, even if you are physically apart.

Additionally, consider using technology to create a shared digital journal where you can both write down your thoughts, prayers, and reflections on your spiritual journey together. This can serve as a meaningful way to document your growth as a couple and support each other in your spiritual practices.

Overall, by incorporating technology into your spiritual practices as a couple, you can strengthen your bond and deepen your connection on a spiritual level, even in the midst of busy schedules and long distances. Embracing these tools can help you both prioritize your faith and prioritize your relationship, leading to a more fulfilling and connected marriage.

Making the Most of Your Time Together When Reunited

In the journey of marriage, there may come times when you and your spouse are separated due to various circumstances such as work, travel, or other commitments. However, when you are finally reunited, it is essential to make the most of your time together to strengthen your bond and connection.

One of the first things you can do when reunited is to prioritize quality time together. Set aside distractions such as work emails, social media, or household chores, and focus solely on each other. Plan activities that you both enjoy and make an effort to engage in meaningful conversations that deepen your emotional intimacy.

Additionally, it is important to show appreciation and affection towards your spouse when you are reunited. Express gratitude for their presence in your life and show physical affection through hugs, kisses, and other gestures of love. Small acts of kindness and thoughtfulness can go a long way in making your time together special.

Furthermore, take the opportunity to engage in spiritual practices together. Whether it is attending religious services, praying together, or reading spiritual texts, connecting on a deeper level spiritually can strengthen your bond as a couple and provide a sense of unity and purpose in your marriage.

In conclusion, when you are finally reunited with your spouse after a period of separation, make the most of your time together by prioritizing quality time, showing appreciation and affection, and engaging in spiritual practices. These actions can help you reconnect, strengthen your bond, and create lasting memories that will sustain your relationship through any challenges that may come your way.

12

Conclusion: Embracing the Spiritual Connection in Your Marriage

In conclusion, embracing the spiritual connection in your marriage can greatly enhance the strength and longevity of your relationship. By prioritizing your faith and spiritual beliefs within your marriage, you are creating a strong foundation built on shared values, trust, and communication.

For couples in interracial marriages, embracing a spiritual connection can help bridge cultural differences and create a sense of unity and understanding. This spiritual bond can serve as a guiding light during times of conflict or hardship, helping to navigate the complexities that may arise in an interracial relationship.

In the realm of marriage counseling, incorporating spirituality into therapy sessions can provide a deeper level of healing and connection for couples. By exploring your faith together, you can uncover underlying issues, gain new perspectives, and strengthen your bond as you work towards a healthier, more fulfilling relationship.

For couples facing challenges in their marriage related to finances, mental health, parenting, infidelity, communication, career, religion/spirituality, or long-distance relationships, embracing a spiritual connection can offer solace and guidance. Whether through prayer, meditation, attending religious services together, or engaging in spiritual practices, finding common ground in your faith can bring you closer together and help you weather the storms that may come your way.

Ultimately, by prioritizing your spiritual connection in your marriage, you are fostering a deep sense of love, understanding, and support that will sustain you through the trials and triumphs of married life. May your faith continue to guide and strengthen your relationship for years to come.